COOKING

THE

ITALIAN

WAY

This book is available in two editions:
Library binding by Lerner Publications Company,
    a division of Lerner Publishing Group
Soft cover by First Avenue Editions,
    an imprint of Lerner Publishing Group
241 First Avenue North
Minneapolis, MN 55401 U.S.A.

Website address: www.lernerbooks.com

Library of Congress Cataloging-in-Publication Data

Bisignano, Alphonse.
    Cooking the Italian way / by Alphonse Bisignano
          p.   cm. — (Easy menu ethnic cookbooks)
    Includes index.
    ISBN 0-8225-4113-0 (lib. bdg. : alk. paper)
    ISBN 0-8225-4161-0 (pbk. : alk. paper)
    1. Cookery, Italian—Juvenile literature. 2. Italy—Social life and
customs—Juvenile literature. [1. Cookery, Italian. 2. Italy—Social
life and customs.] I. Title. II. Series.
TX723.B49 2002   00-009537
641.5945—dc21

Manufactured in the United States of America
1 2 3 4 5 6 – JR – 07 06 05 04 03 02

COOKING

revised and expanded

THE

to include new low-fat

ITALIAN

and vegetarian recipes

WAY

Alphonse Bisignano

Lerner Publications Company • Minneapolis, Minnesota

Contents

Introduction

The words "Italian cooking" make many people think hungrily of pizza, ravioli, and spaghetti smothered in tomato sauce. Juicy tomatoes, cheese, and tasty noodles are certainly used often by Italian cooks. However, there is much more to Italian cuisine.

Heritage and family are two of the most important ingredients in all Italian cooking. Gathering friends and family around the table to share a meal is a highly valued part of social life in Italy. And just as every region of this varied land has a culinary specialty, so does every household and kitchen.

But as traditional as it is, Italian cooking is also very flexible. Most dishes require only a few simple ingredients, and these may vary seasonally and even daily. Italian cooks like to shop every day to ensure that their dishes include only the freshest, most flavorful foods. Whatever is available at the market—and looks the tastiest—will probably determine what is for dinner that day! As the recipes in this book show, colorful fruits and vegetables, olive oil, rice, and fresh herbs make Italian cooking as diverse as it is delicious.

Antipasto *is the perfect beginning for an Italian dinner, offering a variety of fresh ingredients to whet the appetite. (Recipe on page 32.)*

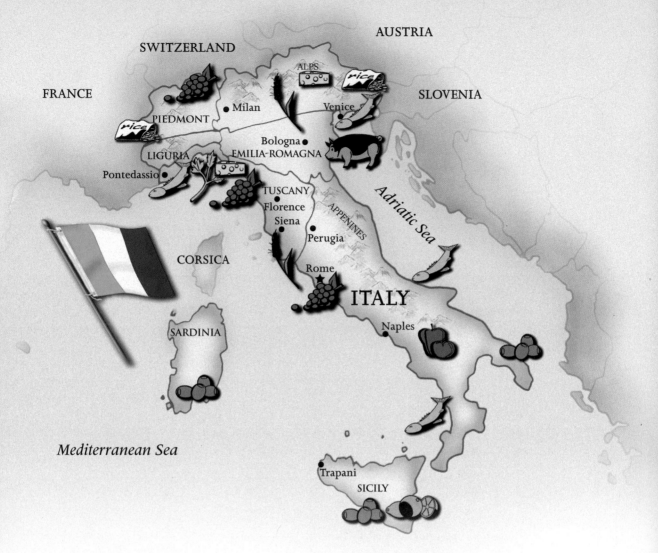

The Land and Its People

Italy is a boot-shaped peninsula that extends into the Mediterranean Sea. The majestic Alps link Italy to the rest of Europe, and the Apennine mountain range runs from the Tuscany region down to the peninsula's southern tip. Many valleys are located in these mountains, and before modern transportation methods, the people who lived there were very isolated. The lack of communication among the Italian people made Italy a divided nation for a long time.

Because the people of each region were loyal to their own area rather than to Italy as a whole, it was easy for other, more powerful nations to take control of the Italian government. Italy passed through periods of Spanish, Austrian, and French rule before becoming an independent country. Not until 1861 did the Italian people become united under one ruler, Victor Emmanuel II.

Even after this unification, however, regional differences remained. The people of each region had developed their own ways of doing things—especially in the kitchen. They were very proud of their distinctive cooking styles and passed down their family recipes from generation to generation.

Regional Cooking

Northern and southern Italy are different from one another. The north has very fertile land and a large, wealthy population, while the south has dry land and a smaller, poorer population. The difference in climate affects the ingredients available for cooking. This fact makes the dishes of northern and southern Italy look and taste distinct from each other. Each of Italy's twenty regions has its own specialties, too.

The northwestern region of Piedmont is known for its fragrant and sparkling wines, and its chief agricultural product is rice. In fact, it is the greatest rice-producing area in Italy, and Italy is Europe's biggest producer of rice. The northeastern regions and the city of Venice are also known for their rice dishes and for their fish dishes. Delicacies such as sole, anchovies, mackerel, eel, spiny lobster, shrimp, and squid from the Adriatic Sea are cooked simply so that their fresh flavor comes through.

The northwestern region of Liguria also uses seafood in its cooking, but it is best known for the use of fragrant herbs. Rosemary, basil, sage, marjoram, and others all decorate Liguria's hillsides. These herbs add special flavors to the dishes of this area.

The main house of a northern Italian estate sits high on a hillside above orchards of fruit trees.

Perhaps the richest cooking is in the north central region of Emilia-Romagna, where butter is the main cooking fat. Emilia-Romagna's specialties include homemade pasta (Emilia-Romagna is Italy's largest producer of wheat), vegetables, fruit, hams, sausages, and rich dairy products, including Parmesan cheese. Bologna, the chief city of that region, is known as *la grassa* (the fat one). It specializes in delicious goose sausages and green lasagna. (For green lasagna, spinach is added to the pasta dough.) Bologna's most famous pork product is mortadella—a smoothly textured, delicately flavored sausage that can be as large as 18 inches around!

South of Emilia-Romagna is the region of Tuscany, whose capital is Florence. This region is known for its use of high-quality ingredients and a minimum of sauces and seasonings. It is simple home cooking at its best.

Italian cooking changes once again south of the Tuscany region. The Apennine Mountains and foothills spread from coast to coast, and olive trees on the hillside replace the fat dairy cows of the north. Olive oil is the dominant cooking fat, and economical, mass-produced, hard macaroni takes the place of soft, homemade pasta.

The city of Naples is known for its pizza, made with thick red tomato sauce and creamy mozzarella cheese. Farther south, as the climate becomes warmer, vegetables have bright, vibrant colors, and pastas are so strongly flavored that a topping is often not needed. Heavy, rich sweets are also enjoyed in the south, particularly in Sicily. This island's volcanic soil is excellent for growing citrus fruits, olives, and grapes.

Holidays and Festivals

No matter what region they come from, Italians love to celebrate. In addition to national holidays, nearly every village and city has its own special festivals. Some festivals honor a patron saint (a saint with special meaning to a particular city), while others celebrate a historical event or a local harvest. But one thing is common to all of these events: food.

Easter, or la Pasqua, is the most important religious holiday for Italy's many Roman Catholics. It is also a time to celebrate the arrival of spring. Many people give their homes an especially good cleaning before Easter. Another custom is to buy new shoes and wear them for the first time on Easter Sunday.

Some cities have special Easter traditions. In Trapani, a town in Sicily, a large procession begins at 2 P.M. on Good Friday (the Friday before Easter Sunday) and lasts all night. Townspeople carry sculptures of the Virgin Mary and other religious figures through the streets, followed by large crowds. On Easter Sunday, a smaller parade includes a figure of Jesus to symbolize his rising from the dead. The city of Florence celebrates with a dramatic fireworks display on Easter Saturday. Pairs of white oxen, with their horns and hooves painted gold, pull a decorated cart through town. In front of the main cathedral, a mechanical dove lights the fireworks on top of the cart. In Rome, thousands of people from all over the world crowd into the square in front of St. Peter's Basilica to hear the pope's Easter Sunday blessing.

A variety of foods is associated with the Easter season. During Lent, the period before Easter, most Italians do not eat certain foods, such as meat and rich desserts. On Good Friday, hot cross buns, which have a cross of white icing on top, are a popular snack. Simple meals of fish or pasta are usually eaten on Good Friday and Easter Saturday. But on Easter Sunday, most families eat a large midday meal. Roast lamb is a traditional main course, representing spring and innocence. Eggs, barley, and wheat are also symbols of spring and rebirth, so breads are a very important part of Italian Easter celebrations. A sweet bread in the shape of a dove, called *la colomba pasquale*, is a popular dessert. People also munch on tiny candy lambs made of sugary almond paste. Hollow chocolate eggs with surprises inside are given as presents to children and adults alike. On Easter Monday, known as Pasquetta, or "little Easter," families go into the countryside for picnics and fun.

Natale, or Christmas, is another important holiday season in Italy. During Advent (a period beginning four Sundays before Christmas), many families make twelve different kinds of cookies, one for each of the twelve days of Christmas (December 25–January 6). During the novena, the nine days before Christmas, shepherds from the mountainous areas of the country often journey into cities such as Rome to play traditional holiday music on bagpipes. Rome also has a famous outdoor market in Piazza Navona, a large city square, where vendors set up stalls selling toys, gifts, and treats.

Italians gather for a Christmas dinner at the Church of San Lorenzo in Rome.

Shoppers snack on hot chestnuts, which are roasted over small stoves and sold in paper cones.

Many Italian cities have large fish markets where cooks can buy the fixings for the Christmas Eve fish dinner on December 24. Traditionally, families eat seven different kinds of seafood, including eel, salted cod, squid, and clams. After the big Christmas Eve meal, kids play *tombola*, a game similar to bingo, until it's time to go to midnight Mass. On Christmas Day, families share another big meal. The menu varies among regions and households, but a typical dish is tortellini in broth. For dessert, many Italians enjoy *panettone*, a special Christmas cake made in Milan.

The Christmas season ends on January 6, or Epiphany. This is the traditional day to exchange gifts in Italy. La Befana, portrayed as an old woman with a broom, brings candy, sweet oranges, and toys to good children. She brings lumps of charcoal to naughty children.

13

Other Italian holidays include Liberation Day, All Souls' Day, New Year's Eve, and New Year's Day. Liberation Day, on April 25, commemorates the Allied victory in Europe at the end of World War II in 1945. This holiday is especially important in Venice because it is also the feast day of Saint Mark, Venice's patron saint. On this day, a dish called *risi e bisi* was traditionally served to the doge, or leader, of Venice. The main ingredients in the dish—which people still eat on this holiday—are rice, to represent prosperity, and peas, to represent spring.

November 2 is All Souls' Day, also called the Day of the Dead. Many Italians visit and decorate graves on this day. Perugia, a city famous for its chocolate, holds the Fair of the Dead, where vendors sell wares and sweets. In Sicily, shops sell sugary treats shaped like skulls. Many families set an extra place at dinner on All Souls' Day to remember friends and family members who have died.

New Year's Eve can be a messy holiday in Italy. As midnight approaches, it is customary to get rid of last year's junk—by throwing it out the window! People may toss old shoes, lamps, or dishes into the street. For good luck in the coming year, Italians eat lentils, which are symbols of wealth because of their coinlike shape. On New Year's Day, people often exchange good-luck gifts of mistletoe and calendars. Lasagna is a typical main course for dinner.

Unlike national holidays, which are recognized all over Italy, festivals are usually celebrated only by certain towns or regions. For example, the Palio is a traditional horse race in Siena each August 16. The festival honors the city's patron saint and dates back to the Middle Ages. Siena is divided into contrade, or neighborhoods, which compete against each other in the Palio. The night before the race, the contrade hold elaborate good-luck feasts. The next day, each horse is blessed by a priest, and then a great pageant of trumpets, banners, and townspeople dressed in bright medieval costumes parades to the racetrack. The track runs around Piazza del Campo, Siena's central square. Although the race is very short—it is usually over in less than two minutes—it can be quite dangerous.

Mattresses pad the walls near sharp turns and steep hills, since riders are often thrown from their horses.

Afterward, the winners of the Palio celebrate by serving free wine to everyone. The winning contrada also hosts a huge banquet a few weeks later for thousands of guests. A traditional dish at this feast is a risotto served with Siena's local sausage. Of course, the winning horse has a place of honor and munches on oats and sugar cubes.

Venice's Regata Storica is very similar to a Palio. This early September festival is also a race—but the competitors are in boats rather than on horses. Gondole, traditional Venetian boats for navigating the city's many canals, are rowed up and down the Grand Canal by people in historical dress. After the race, everyone enjoys a big meal, at which squash soup is a typical dish.

Food plays a large role in Italian life and culture, so it is no surprise that many festivals celebrate particular foods. Called *sagre*, these events often take place at harvesttime and usually include dancing, live music, and lots of eating. For example, in late October, many areas in northern Italy celebrate the ripening of the chestnuts. In one town, people gather in the chestnut groves and shake the trees to make more nuts fall. Then they gather them up and create all kinds of tasty dishes, such as soups, tarts, cakes, and pastas.

Wherever olives are grown and olive oil is made, sagre are held in honor of the late autumn olive harvest. A traditional food at these sagre is *bruschetta*. A simple bruschetta is lightly toasted Italian bread topped with olive oil, garlic, salt, and pepper. However, cooks may add tomatoes, anchovies, or truffles to their own recipes for even more flavor.

Italy, and especially the region of Liguria, is famous for basil. The Ligurian town of Pontedassio holds a basil festival in early June. Citizens sample a variety of dishes, many of them featuring pesto, a delicious mixture of basil, pine nuts, Parmesan cheese, and olive oil.

Dozens of other sagre throughout Italy feature foods as varied as fish, grapes, cheeses, and pastas. But everywhere, in every season, Italians are sure to celebrate the joys of a good meal in good company.

At a market in Venice, shoppers buy produce for the day's meal.

An Italian Market

Throughout Italy, cooks enjoy a wealth of fine, fresh vegetables. Each city or town has an outdoor market, usually located near the main piazza (square) or cathedral. The vegetable stalls found on dusty side streets are ablaze with the colors of Italy's finest produce—red tomatoes, green zucchini, purple eggplants, and bright orange carrots are artistically displayed.

In the spring and fall, fresh wild mushrooms take their place alongside the vegetables. Brown, orange, and cream-colored varieties can all be found, and Italians find each a special seasonal treat.

Hanging above the produce, festoons of dried and fresh herbs wave in the breeze. Bunches of parsley, basil, marjoram, thyme, rosemary, and other herbs are bought at the market and brought home to become an indispensable part of the Italian kitchen. Also hanging from market stalls are abundant poultry and game. Ducks, geese, chickens, and turkeys are ready for each shopper's inspection, and in some areas, deer and wild boar are available as well.

After a morning at the market, shoppers both young and old find the local ice cream vendor a welcome sight. Italy has perhaps the best ice cream in the world. *Gelato* is a milk-based ice cream that is much like the chocolate and vanilla ice cream found in North America, and *granita* is a light sherbet made of ice and syrup. Popular flavors include coffee, lemon, and strawberry. Each is sure to disappear deliciously the second it touches the tongue!

To finish their shopping, Italian cooks may stop at a pastry shop, or *pasticceria*. There they can buy pastries, which Italians eat in midmorning or midafternoon rather than after a meal. More elaborate sweets are reserved for special occasions, and each region of Italy has its own favorite. Rome, for example, relishes a smooth ricotta cheese pie, southern Italy enjoys chewy macaroons, and Milan's panettone is so popular that it is even exported to the United States.

Before You Begin

Cooking any dish, plain or fancy, is easier and more fun if you are familiar with the ingredients and the preparation. Italian cooking calls for some ingredients that you may not know. Sometimes special cookware is also used, although the recipes in this book can easily be prepared with ordinary utensils and pans.

The most important thing you need to know before you start is how to be a careful cook. On the following page, you'll find a few rules that will make your cooking experience safe, fun, and easy. Next, take a look at the "dictionary" of terms and special ingredients. You may also want to read the list of tips on preparing healthy, low-fat meals for yourself, your family, and your friends.

Once you've picked out a recipe to try, read through it from beginning to end. Now you are ready to shop for ingredients and to organize the cookware you will need. When you have assembled everything, you're ready to begin cooking.

The blend of tomato, garlic, and green pepper in pollo alla cacciatore *is typical of Italian country cooking. Warm up with this hearty dish on a cool day! (Recipe on page 47.)*

The Careful Cook

Whenever you cook, there are certain safety rules you must always keep in mind. Even experienced cooks follow these rules when they are in the kitchen.

- Always wash your hands before handling food. Thoroughly wash all raw vegetables and fruits to remove dirt, chemicals, and insecticides. Wash uncooked poultry, fish, and meat under cold water.
- Use a cutting board when cutting up vegetables and fruits. Don't cut them up in your hand! And be sure to cut in a direction *away* from you and your fingers.
- Long hair or loose clothing can easily catch fire if brought near the burners of a stove. If you have long hair, tie it back before you start cooking.
- Turn all pot handles toward the back of the stove so that you will not catch your sleeves or jewelry on them. This is especially important when younger brothers and sisters are around. They could easily knock off a pot and get burned.
- Always use a pot holder to steady hot pots or to take pans out of the oven. Don't use a wet cloth on a hot pan because the steam it produces could burn you.
- Lift the lid of a steaming pot with the opening away from you so that you will not get burned.
- If you get burned, hold the burn under cold running water. Do not put grease or butter on it. Cold water helps to take the heat out, but grease or butter will only keep it in.
- If grease or cooking oil catches fire, throw baking soda or salt at the bottom of the flame to put it out. (Water will *not* put out a grease fire.) Call for help, and try to turn all the stove burners to "off."

Cooking Utensils

colander—A bowl-shaped dish with holes in it that is used for washing or draining food

Dutch oven—A heavy pot with a tight-fitting domed cover that is often used for cooking soups or stews

Cooking Terms

al dente—An Italian cooking term, literally meaning "to the tooth," that describes the point at which pasta is properly cooked—firm and tender to bite, but not soft

boil—To heat a liquid over high heat until bubbles form and rise rapidly to the surface

brown—To cook food quickly in fat over high heat so that the surface turns an even brown

dice—To chop food into small, square-shaped pieces

fold—To blend an ingredient with other ingredients by using a gentle overturning circular motion instead of by stirring or beating

grate—To cut food into tiny pieces by rubbing it against a grater

hard-cook—To boil an egg in its shell until both the yolk and white are firm

mince—To chop food into very small pieces

preheat—To allow an oven to warm up to a certain temperature before putting food in it

sauté—To fry quickly over high heat in oil or fat, stirring or turning the food to prevent burning

shred—To tear or cut into small pieces, either by hand or with a grater

simmer—To cook over low heat in liquid kept just below its boiling point. Bubbles may occasionally rise to the surface.

Special Ingredients

almond extract—A liquid made from the oil of the almond nut and used to give an almond flavor to food

artichoke—An herb with a green, thistlelike head that is eaten as a vegetable. The tender center of the artichoke, called the heart, has a delicate flavor and is often used in salads. Canned artichoke hearts are packed in either water or oil and vinegar.

basil—A rich and fragrant herb whose leaves are used in cooking

bay leaf—The dried leaf of the bay (also called laurel) tree. It is used to season food.

CHEESES

mozzarella—A moist, white, unsalted cheese with a mild flavor and a smooth, rubbery texture

Parmesan—A hard, dry, sharply flavored Italian cheese

pimento cheese—A cheese to which chopped pimientos have been added

provolone—A creamy, yellow Italian cheese with a mild flavor

ricotta—A soft, creamy, unsalted Italian cheese that is similar in texture to cream cheese but more like cottage cheese in flavor

Romano—A hard Italian cheese with a sharper flavor than Parmesan

dry mustard—A powder, made from the ground seeds of the mustard plant, that is used to flavor food

garlic—An herb whose distinctive flavor is used in many dishes. Fresh garlic can usually be found in the produce department of a supermarket. Each piece or bulb can be broken up into several small sections called cloves. Most recipes use only one or two finely chopped cloves of this very strong herb. Before you chop up a clove of garlic, you will have to peel off the brittle, papery covering that surrounds it.

Italian sausage—A sausage made from ground pork, seasonings, and preservatives and packed into an edible casing *maraschino cherries*—Large cherries preserved in a sweet liquid

nutmeg—A fragrant spice, either whole or ground, that is often used in desserts and cheese sauces

olive oil—An oil made from pressed olives that is used in cooking and for dressing salads

oregano—The dried leaves, whole or powdered, of a rich and fragrant herb that is used as a seasoning in cooking

paprika—A red seasoning made from ground, dried pods of the capsicum pepper plant

PASTAS

    elbow macaroni—Smooth, curved, tube-shaped noodles about 1 inch long

    fettucini—Noodles in the form of narrow ribbons

    linguine—Thin, flat noodles

    mostaccioli—Ridged, tube-shaped noodles about 2 inches long

    rigatoni—Short, slightly curved, fluted noodles

    spaghetti—Noodles made in the form of long, thin strands

    spinach noodles—Noodles, made with spinach, that are green in color

    tortellini—Pasta that has been cut into rounds, filled with cheese, meat, or other filling, folded in half, and formed into rings

prosciutto—Dry, cured ham that is pale red in color and has a delicate, sweet flavor

scallions—Another name for green onions

yeast—An ingredient used in baking that causes dough to rise and become light and fluffy. Yeast is available in either small, white cakes called compressed yeast or in granular form called active dry yeast.

Healthy and Low-Fat Cooking Tips

Many modern cooks are concerned about preparing healthy, low-fat meals. Fortunately, there are simple ways to reduce the fat content of most dishes. Here are a few general tips for adapting the recipes in this book. Throughout the book, you'll also find specific suggestions for individual recipes—and don't worry, they'll still taste delicious!

Many recipes call for butter or oil to sauté vegetables or other ingredients. Using oil lowers fat right away, but you can also reduce the amount of oil you use. Sprinkling a little salt on the vegetables brings out their natural juices, so less oil is needed. It's also a good idea to use a small, nonstick frying pan if you decide to use less oil than the recipe calls for.

Another common substitution for butter is margarine. Before making this substitution, consider the recipe. If it is a dessert, it's often best to use butter. Margarine may noticeably change the taste or consistency of the food.

Cheese is a common source of unwanted fat. Many cheeses are available in reduced or nonfat varieties, but keep in mind that these varieties often don't melt as well. Another easy way to reduce the amount of fat from cheese is simply to use less of it! To avoid losing flavor, you might try using a stronger-tasting cheese.

Some cooks like to replace ground beef with ground turkey to lower fat. However, since this does change the flavor, you may need to experiment a little bit to decide if you like this substitution. Buying extra-lean ground beef is also an easy way to reduce fat.

There are many ways to prepare meals that are good for you and still taste great. As you become a more experienced cook, try experimenting with recipes and substitutions to find the methods that work best for you.

METRIC CONVERSIONS

Cooks in the United States measure both liquid and solid ingredients using standard containers based on the 8-ounce cup and the tablespoon. These measurements are based on volume, while the metric system of measurement is based on both weight (for solids) and volume (for liquids). To convert from U.S. fluid tablespoons, ounces, quarts, and so forth to metric liters is a straightforward conversion, using the chart below. However, since solids have different weights—one cup of rice does not weigh the same as one cup of grated cheese, for example—many cooks who use the metric system have kitchen scales to weigh different ingredients. The chart below will give you a good starting point for basic conversions to the metric system.

MASS (weight)

1 ounce (oz.)	=	28.0 grams (g)
8 ounces	=	227.0 grams
1 pound (lb.) or 16 ounces	=	0.45 kilograms (kg)
2.2 pounds	=	1.0 kilogram

LIQUID VOLUME

1 teaspoon (tsp.)	=	5.0 milliliters (ml)
1 tablespoon (tbsp.)	=	15.0 milliliters
1 fluid ounce (oz.)	=	30.0 milliliters
1 cup (c.)	=	240 milliliters
1 pint (pt.)	=	480 milliliters
1 quart (qt.)	=	0.95 liters (l)
1 gallon (gal.)	=	3.80 liters

LENGTH

¼ inch (in.)	=	0.6 centimeters (cm)
½ inch	=	1.25 centimeters
1 inch	=	2.5 centimeters

TEMPERATURE

212°F	=	100°C (boiling point of water)
225°F	=	110°C
250°F	=	120°C
275°F	=	135°C
300°F	=	150°C
325°F	=	160°C
350°F	=	180°C
375°F	=	190°C
400°F	=	200°C

(To convert temperature in Fahrenheit to Celsius, subtract 32 and multiply by .56)

PAN SIZES

8-inch cake pan	=	20 x 4-centimeter cake pan
9-inch cake pan	=	23 x 3.5-centimeter cake pan
11 x 7-inch baking pan	=	28 x 18-centimeter baking pan
13 x 9-inch baking pan	=	32.5 x 23-centimeter baking pan
9 x 5-inch loaf pan	=	23 x 13-centimeter loaf pan
2-quart casserole	=	2-liter casserole

An Italian Table

An Italian dining table is generally covered with a fine linen table-cloth. A bowl of fresh fruit provides color, as does the bottle of wine that is usually present at every meal except breakfast. Diners help themselves to slices from the large hunks of cheese, rolls of sausage, and loaves of bread (always served without butter) that are often placed on the table.

A small glass filled with toothpicks is another familiar sight on an Italian table. The Italian word for toothpicks is *stuzzicadenti*, but the Italians have labeled them *l'ultimo piatto*, or "the last course."

The Italian table is set with all of the silver and glasses to be used during the meal. Each diner sits before a flat plate with a soup plate placed on top of it. The soup or pasta is served into the top dish, which is then removed for the following courses. Italians always eat their meals in stages—one course at a time.

In an Italian home, eating is a leisurely affair. Family members of all ages gather around the table to enjoy a delicious meal. Italian cooks take pride in presenting their finest dishes to their families and close friends. When you learn how to make the recipes in this book, you can do the same.

Italians enjoy sitting outside at restaurants and cafés to dine and to watch passersby.

An Italian Menu

Although many Italians have a hearty diet and eat three meals a day, breakfast is usually a small meal and may only consist of a cup of coffee and maybe a pastry. Below are menu plans for a typical Italian dinner and supper, together with shopping lists of items that you will need to prepare these meals.* All the recipes are found in this book.

DINNER

Antipasto with dressing

Straw and hay

Chicken hunter's style

Italian-style cauliflower

Fresh fruit

SHOPPING LIST:

Produce

1 head Boston or
   romaine lettuce
6 carrots
celery
2 tomatoes
1 bunch radishes
1 bunch scallions
1 head garlic
½–¾ lb. fresh mushrooms
1 onion
2 green peppers
1 head fresh cauliflower
fresh fruit
2½–3 lb. eggplant (if not
   buying chicken)

Dairy/Egg/Meat

6 slices provolone or
   mozzarella cheese
eggs
2 sticks butter
½ pt. whipping cream
Parmesan cheese
milk

1 lb. mild pimento cheese
2½–3 lb. chicken pieces
   (if not buying eggplant)
6 slices salami

Canned/Bottled/Boxed

1 can artichoke hearts
black and green olives
olive oil
white wine vinegar
lemon juice
thin spinach noodles
fettucini noodles
1 small can tiny peas
1 8-oz. can stewed tomatoes

Miscellaneous

salt
pepper
sugar
flour
dry mustard
paprika
oregano
basil

SUPPER

Pizza

Green salad

Biscuit tortoni

SHOPPING LIST:

Produce

1 head garlic
1 onion
1 green pepper
lettuce for green salad
pizza toppings (see page
    55 for ideas)

Dairy

8 oz. grated mozzarella
½ pt. whipping cream
    or 1 qt. frozen yogurt

Canned/Bottled/Boxed

1 envelope active dry yeast
1 6-oz. can tomato paste
1 16-oz. can whole tomatoes
maraschino cherries
olive oil
almonds
macaroon cookies
dressing for green salad

Miscellaneous

almond extract
salt
flour
oregano
basil
sugar

*If you plan to do a lot of Italian cooking, you may want to stock up
on some of the items on these shopping lists and keep them on hand.
Garlic, olive oil, pasta, and canned tomatoes all keep well and are
common ingredients in many Italian dishes.

Dinner / Il Pranzo

By 12:00 P.M., most Italians who have breakfasted lightly are ready for a big dinner with several courses. There is no main course in an Italian meal. Instead, there are at least two principal courses that are never brought to the table at the same time. The meal usually starts with the antipasto, or appetizer. The purpose of this plate is to get the diner's stomach ready for the soup, which is followed by the pasta. After the pasta, the course of meat or fish is served, along with side dishes of cooked vegetables. The vegetables often reflect the colors of the season. Early peas and asparagus are found on a table in springtime, cauliflower and artichokes are winter fare, and bright tomatoes, eggplants, and green peppers liven up summer meals.

Italians generally drink wine with their meals. (Even the children in Italy drink wine, although it is diluted with water or soda pop.) Dessert in Italy is usually a piece of fruit, which is always cut into small pieces before it is eaten. It "clears the palate" and cleans the teeth. After the meal, Italians may enjoy a strong black coffee called espresso. Coffee time, however, is generally at about 4:00 P.M. At that time, cups of either espresso or cappuccino are served. Cappuccino is espresso with a layer of steamed milk on top.

Pasta Cinese *is a hearty baked pasta dish. Serve with crusty bread and a green salad. (Recipe on page 36.)*

Appetizer / Antipasto

Antipasto is an Italian word that comes from Latin. Ante means "before" and pasto means "pasta" or "dough." Antipasto is, therefore, what diners eat before the pasta.*

several leaves of lettuce

½ head fresh greens, such as Boston or romaine lettuce, shredded

6 carrots, peeled, halved lengthwise, and cut into 3-inch pieces

6 celery stalks, cut into 3-inch pieces

6 salami slices

6 provolone or mozzarella cheese slices

2 tomatoes

2 hard-cooked eggs

6 canned artichoke hearts

black and green olives for garnish

radishes for garnish

1 bunch of scallions for garnish

¼ c. Italian salad dressing (recipe follows)

1. Wash all fresh vegetables thoroughly and let dry.

2. Cover a large serving plate with leaf lettuce. Place shredded greens on top.

3. Divide carrot and celery sticks in half and place at each end of the plate.

4. In the center of the plate, lay alternate slices of salami and cheese.

5. Cut tomatoes and hard-cooked eggs into quarters. Arrange egg and tomato quarters and artichoke hearts around the edge of the plate.

6. Place olives, a few radishes, and some scallions wherever they fit in attractively. (Any other fresh raw vegetables such as broccoli or cauliflower cut into bite-sized pieces may be added.)

7. Dribble salad dressing over all.

Preparation time: 20 minutes
Serves 6 to 8

Italian Salad Dressing/
Condimento Italiano per Insalata

1 c. olive oil

¼ c. white wine vinegar

2 tbsp. lemon juice

1 tsp. salt

½ tsp. pepper

1 tsp. sugar

½ tsp. dry mustard

¼ tsp. paprika

½ tsp. oregano

⅛ tsp. basil

1 clove garlic, crushed

1. Combine all ingredients in a tightly covered jar. Shake well until dressing is thoroughly mixed.

2. Refrigerate for 2 hours. Shake well before serving.

Preparation time: 5 minutes
Chilling time: 2 hours
Makes 1 ½ cups

To serve a lighter antipasto, you may choose to add more vegetables and omit or reduce the amount of meat and cheese. Also try varying the ratios of ingredients in the dressing. For example, to make a refreshing, zingy dressing, use only ½ c. olive oil and increase the amount of lemon juice to ½ c.

Minestrone

Minestrone is a rich, thick vegetable soup. It gets its name from the Latin word minestrare, which means "to serve" or "to dish up."

1 16-oz. can kidney beans

1 clove garlic, minced

½ tsp. salt

¼ tsp. pepper

1 tbsp. olive oil

¼ c. chopped fresh parsley

1 small fresh zucchini, unpeeled and diced

2 celery stalks with leaves, finely chopped

2 small carrots, peeled and diced

1 small onion, minced

1 16-oz. can whole tomatoes, cut up with a spoon

2½ c. water

⅓ c. elbow macaroni, uncooked

½ c. beef bouillon or tomato juice

salt to taste

1. Put beans in a large kettle and mash them slightly with a fork.

2. Add garlic, salt, pepper, oil, and parsley. Stir well.

3. Add water and all vegetables to the kettle.* Bring to a boil over medium heat, stirring occasionally.

4. Lower heat, cover the kettle, and simmer 1 hour, stirring occasionally.

5. After 1 hour, add macaroni and beef bouillon or tomato juice. Simmer 15 minutes, stirring occasionally. Add salt to taste.

Preparation time: 20 minutes
Cooking time: 2½ hours
Serves 6 to 8

*For an even more substantial soup, try adding 3 medium red potatoes, peeled and diced, 1 c. shredded cabbage, and/or 1 c. frozen green beans, thawed.

Full of veggies, minestrone is a flavorful soup that can be a satisfying low-fat meal in itself.

Chinese Pasta/ *Pasta Cinese*

As with any pasta dish, this one is quite filling and can be eaten as a meal in itself. For Pasta Cinese, you will make a sauce and meatballs that can be used in other dishes or served alone as a side dish.

Sauce ingredients:

1 12-oz. can tomato paste

3 c. water

1 tsp. basil

1 tsp. oregano

1 large bay leaf

1 clove garlic, minced

1 medium-sized onion, chopped

1 tsp. salt

dash of pepper

2 or 3 Italian sausage links (optional)

1. Combine all ingredients in a Dutch oven. Cover and simmer over low heat for 2 hours, stirring occasionally.* (If sauce becomes too thick and begins to stick to the sides of the pot, add a little water.)

2. Remove the lid about 15 minutes before serving so that the sauce can thicken. (Sauce should be heavy and smooth.)

Preparation time: 5 minutes
Cooking time: 2 hours
Makes 1 qt. of sauce

*While the sauce is simmering for 2 hours, you will have plenty of time to make the meatballs and cook the pasta.

Meatball ingredients:

½ lb. lean ground beef

½ c. cracker or bread crumbs

1 egg

pinch of oregano

pinch of basil

1. Put all ingredients except oil in a large bowl and mix well. (Many cooks use their hands for mixing meatballs.)

2. Roll about 1 tbsp. meat between the palms of your hands to make meatballs that are ¾ inch in diameter.

salt to taste

pepper to taste

I clove garlic, minced

I small onion, finely chopped

2 tbsp. grated Romano or
   Parmesan cheese

vegetable oil for frying

Pasta ingredients:

8 oz. mostaccioli or rigatoni
   noodles, uncooked

I qt. sauce

25 to 30 small meatballs

I or 2 hard-cooked eggs, sliced

½ c. grated mozzarella cheese

dash of grated Romano or
   Parmesan cheese

3. In a frying pan, brown meatballs in about ½ inch of oil. Drain. (Or place meatballs in a shallow pan and bake at 350°F for about 10 minutes.)

Preparation time: 20 minutes
Cooking time: 10 to 15 minutes
Makes 25 to 30 small meatballs

1. Boil noodles according to directions on package and drain.

2. Preheat the oven to 350°F.

3. In a square 8 × 8-inch baking dish or cake pan, layer ingredients in the following order: a small amount of sauce on the bottom; then noodles, meatballs, and egg slices; then another layer of sauce, topped with mozzarella cheese. (Save some sauce to pour over each portion after baking.)

4. Sprinkle with Romano or Parmesan cheese and bake for 20 minutes or until bubbling and heated through.

5. When done, remove Chinese Pasta from the oven and let cool slightly before cutting into squares for serving. Pour remaining sauce over each serving.

Preparation time: 25 minutes
Cooking time: 20 minutes
Serves 4 to 6

Straw and Hay / *Paglia e Fieno*

These creamy noodles originated in the city of Siena, which still has the look of the Middle Ages. The green noodles are the "hay," and the white noodles are the "straw." For a tasty variation, sauté 1 c. thinly sliced cooked ham with the peas and mushrooms and serve the finished dish as a main course.

4 oz. thin spinach noodles, uncooked

4 oz. fettucini noodles, uncooked

3 tbsp. butter

1 clove garlic, minced

½ c. canned tiny peas, drained (optional)

¼ lb. fresh mushrooms, sliced

¾ c. whipping cream

½ tsp. salt

pepper to taste

¼ c. grated Parmesan cheese

1. Cook noodles in boiling salted water until they are al dente. Drain and toss with half the butter. Cover and set aside.

2. Melt remaining butter in a large saucepan. Sauté garlic until golden. Spoon out garlic and discard.

3. In the same butter, sauté peas and mushrooms over low heat for 5 minutes. At the same time, heat cream in a small pan. (Do not boil.)

4. Add noodles, cream, salt, and pepper to vegetables in the large saucepan. With the pan still over low heat, toss vigorously with a long handled spoon and fork.

5. Remove from heat and quickly stir in cheese. Serve on warm plates. Pass more grated Parmesan cheese at the table.

Preparation time: 15 minutes
Cooking time: 30 minutes
Serves 4

Colorful spinach noodles and fresh mushrooms make paglia e fieno (straw and hay) a treat for the eyes as well as the tongue.

Risotto

Risotto is a creamy delicacy made with white rice. If you like to stir, you'll like preparing this dish.

2 to 2½ 15-oz. cans chicken broth

4 tbsp. butter

2 tbsp. vegetable oil

2 tbsp. minced onion

1½ c. white rice, uncooked*

⅔ c. grated Parmesan cheese

1. Heat broth until simmering.

2. In a heavy saucepan, heat 2 tbsp. butter with the oil. Sauté onion in butter and oil until golden.

3. Add rice and stir until well coated. Sauté rice briefly, then add ½ c. of the simmering broth. Cook over medium heat, stirring constantly, until rice absorbs liquid. Then add another ½ c. broth. Continue cooking and stirring, adding another ½ c. broth each time rice dries out. (This will take about 30 minutes. When finished, rice will be creamy and tender, yet firm.)

4. When rice is almost done, add grated cheese and remaining butter. If needed, season with a little salt. Serve immediately. Pass more grated Parmesan cheese at the table.

*Arborio rice, a polished short-grain Italian rice, is the best kind to use for risotto because of its creamy texture when cooked. Most Italian groceries and some supermarkets carry Arborio rice. But if you can't find it, you can substitute another white, short-grain variety.

Preparation time: 10 minutes
Cooking time: 40 minutes
Serves 6

Spaghetti with Meat Sauce / Spaghetti al Sugo

1 15-oz. can tomato sauce

1 12-oz. can tomato paste

⅔ c. water

1 small onion, finely chopped

1 clove garlic, minced

1 3-oz. can mushroom pieces
   and liquid

½ tsp. nutmeg

¼ c. sugar

1 lb. lean ground beef*

½ c. tomato juice or water

½ c. grated Parmesan cheese

8 oz. spaghetti noodles, uncooked

*Ground beef can easily be omitted
from spaghetti al sugo for a
delicious vegetarian dish.

1. Combine tomato sauce, tomato paste, water, onion, garlic, mushrooms with liquid, nutmeg, and sugar in a Dutch oven.

2. Bring to a boil on top of the stove. Meanwhile, preheat the oven to 250°F.

3. Cover and cook sauce in the oven for 2 hours. (Sauce can be cooked on top of the stove if simmered very slowly.)

4. After 2 hours, add ground beef. (You can crumble it into the sauce or shape it into meatballs about 1 inch in diameter.) Cook 1 hour.

5. Add tomato juice or water and cheese and cook for 20 minutes.

6. While sauce is cooking, prepare spaghetti al dente, following directions on package. (Be careful not to overcook spaghetti. Overcooked spaghetti will probably be too soft and will stick together.)

7. Drain spaghetti and place on a deep platter. Cover with sauce and serve.

Preparation time: 25 minutes
Cooking time: 3 hours 20 minutes
Serves 4 to 6

Italian-Style Pork Chops/
Costolette di Maiale Italiano

4 pork chops, about 1 inch thick

salt and pepper to taste

1 garlic clove, minced

1½ tbsp. olive or vegetable oil

½ c. canned tomato sauce

1 green pepper, cleaned out
    and cut into thin strips

¼ lb. fresh mushrooms, sliced,
    or 1 3-oz. can mushroom
    pieces, drained

¾ tsp. oregano

¼ c. tomato juice

4 oz. hot Italian sausage (optional)

1. Trim excess fat from pork chops and wash chops under cold water.

2. Mix salt, pepper, and garlic in a bowl. Rub on pork chops.

3. Heat oil in large skillet and brown chops on both sides.

4. Add tomato sauce, green pepper, mushrooms, oregano, and tomato juice to the skillet. Cover and cook over low heat for about 30 minutes. (If you add sausage, brown it in a separate pan and drain. Add to the skillet during the last 10 minutes of cooking.)

5. Spoon sauce over chops and serve.

Preparation time: 20 minutes
Cooking time: 45 minutes
Serves 4

Spicy sausage can add a bit of zip to Italian-style pork chops.

Chicken Hunter's Style / *Pollo alla Cacciatore*

1 2½- to 3-lb. chicken, cut into serving pieces*

¼ c. butter

2 tbsp. olive or vegetable oil

1 c. finely chopped onion

½ green pepper, cleaned out and chopped

2 garlic cloves, minced

½ tsp. basil

1 tsp. salt

½ tsp. pepper

1 c. stewed tomatoes, undrained

½ c. tomato juice, canned chicken broth, or water

sliced mushrooms for garnish (optional)

1. In a large skillet, brown chicken in butter and oil over medium heat until pieces are evenly brown on all sides.

2. Add onion, green pepper, garlic, basil, salt, and pepper. Stir. Cook until onion is soft but not brown (about 5 minutes).

3. Add undrained tomatoes and stir well. Bring to a boil, cover, and cook over low heat for 20 minutes, stirring occasionally.

4. Add tomato juice, chicken broth, or water and simmer 10 minutes.

5. Remove chicken to serving dish and spoon sauce over chicken. Garnish with mushroom slices, if desired.

Preparation time: 15 minutes
Cooking time: 45 minutes
Serves 4

*Substituting eggplant for chicken turns this into a delicious vegetarian entrée. Slice 2 medium eggplants lengthwise and lightly coat with olive oil. Place cut-side down on a cookie sheet and roast in the oven at 400°F for about 20 minutes or until tender and easy to pierce with a fork. Remove, cut into bite-sized chunks, and cover with sauce. Pollo alla cacciatore has become melanzane alla cacciatore!

Serve pollo alla cacciatore *with fresh Italian bread for a simple but tasty combination.*

Bisignano Spinach / *Spinaci Bisignano*

2 10-oz. packages frozen chopped spinach, cooked, or 1½ lbs. fresh spinach, cooked and finely chopped

1 16-oz. carton ricotta or cottage cheese*

1 c. bread crumbs or packaged herb stuffing

2 eggs, lightly beaten

¼ c. sliced fresh mushrooms or canned sliced mushrooms, drained

½ c. chopped green pepper

1 c. sour cream

½ c. spaghetti sauce, canned or homemade (see page 36)

1 lb. mozzarella cheese, sliced

1 tsp. basil

½ c. grated Parmesan cheese

1. In a large bowl, combine spinach, ricotta or cottage cheese, bread crumbs, eggs, mushrooms, and green pepper.

2. Preheat the oven to 350°F.

3. Pour mixture into a buttered 9×13-inch baking dish and spread sour cream on top.

4. Pour on a layer of spaghetti sauce, using most, but not all, of sauce. Cover with a layer of mozzarella cheese slices.

5. Spread remaining spaghetti sauce over cheese slices. Sprinkle with basil and Parmesan cheese.

6. Bake for 30 minutes.

Preparation time: 25 minutes
Cooking time: 30 minutes
Serves 6 to 8

*To lower the fat content of Bisignano Spinach, use reduced-fat ricotta or cottage cheese, reduced-fat sour cream, and only ½ lb. thinly sliced mozzarella.

Italian-Style Cauliflower/*Cavolfiore Italiano*

1 head fresh cauliflower*

4 tbsp. butter or margarine

1 small green pepper, cleaned out
and sliced

¼ lb. fresh mushrooms, sliced

2 tbsp. all-purpose flour

1 c. milk

1 lb. mild pimento cheese, sliced

1. Cut core out of cauliflower and
place its flower-shaped pieces in a
large kettle of water. Bring water to
a boil and cook cauliflower about 3
to 5 minutes. Drain.

2. Melt butter in a skillet and sauté
pepper slices and mushrooms.

3. Preheat the oven to 350°F.

4. Remove the skillet from heat and
sprinkle in flour a little at a time,
stirring briskly.

5. Add milk slowly, stirring constantly.
Return to heat and stir until mixture
thickens.

6. Place cauliflower in a casserole dish.
Lay cheese slices over cauliflower
and pour creamed green pepper and
mushrooms over the top. Bake 20
minutes.

Preparation time: 20 minutes
Cooking time: 35 to 40 minutes
Serves 6

*When choosing fresh cauliflower, look
for heads that are firm and very white,
with crisp, green leaves. Avoid heads
with brown spots or yellowish,
wilted leaves. To store cauliflower for
a couple of days, just cover the whole
head with plastic wrap and put it
in the refrigerator.*

Supper / La Cena

An Italian supper is generally smaller than the hearty midday meal, but it is just as satisfying and delicious. It may consist of a nice thick soup, pizza, green salad, and fresh fruit or a light sweet for dessert. Since many households in Italy have their own orchards and gardens, most families enjoy a wide variety of fresh fruits and vegetables daily

When a family goes to a restaurant to eat supper, it is common to see young children with their heads down on the table, fast asleep. Italians usually eat supper at about 8:00 P.M., and they consider it very important to relax and not hurry through the meal. They may not be done eating until 10:00 P.M. or even later, so it's not surprising that the children sometimes have a hard time staying awake while the adults finish their supper.

An Italian favorite, pizza is a fun and easy dish that you can adapt to your personal tastes. (Recipe on page 54.)

Pizza

Cooks put almost anything on pizza. Pizza Margherita, a popular variety in Italy, was first made in 1889 for Queen Margherita and King Umberto I. It is topped with the colors of the Italian flag: fresh red tomatoes, green basil leaves, and creamy white mozzarella. See page 55 for a few toppings that you might like to try on your pizza. Be creative and add your own favorites to the list.

Pizza ingredients:

1 envelope active dry yeast

1 c. warm water

½ tsp. salt

2 tbsp. olive or vegetable oil

2½ c. all-purpose flour

pizza sauce (recipe follows)

8 oz. mozzarella cheese, grated

desired pizza toppings (suggestions follow)

1. Dissolve yeast in 1 cup warm water. Stir in salt and oil. Gradually stir in flour. Beat vigorously 20 strokes. Let dough rest about 5 minutes.

2. Put dough in a warm place, cover with a damp towel, and let rise until double in size (about 45 minutes).

3. Punch dough down with your fist to let out the air. Divide dough in half.

4. Lightly grease 2 baking sheets or 2 10-inch pizza pans. With floured fingers, pat each half of the dough into a 10-inch circle.* Build up edges of pizzas with your fingers to keep sauce from running off.

5. Spread pizza sauce over dough. Sprinkle with grated cheese and your favorite toppings.

6. Bake at 425°F for 20 to 25 minutes. Let pizzas stand at least 5 minutes before cutting.

*Dough should be thinly and evenly spread with no holes in it. For a thicker crust, use 2 9-inch cake pans.

Preparation time: 15 minutes
Rising time: 30 to 45 minutes
Baking time: 20 to 25 minutes
Serves 4 to 6

No-cook pizza sauce:

1 6-oz. can tomato paste

1 16-oz.can whole tomatoes,
   cut up with a spoon

2 cloves garlic, minced

1 tsp. oregano

1 tsp. basil

1 tsp. olive or vegetable oil

¼ c. minced onion

1 green pepper, cleaned out and
   minced (optional)

1. In a large bowl, mix all ingredients together with a fork.

2. Spoon sauce onto unbaked pizza crust. Add topping, if desired, and bake as directed in basic recipe on page 54.

Preparation time: 15 minutes
Enough for 2 pizzas

Pizza toppings:

anchovies

artichoke hearts

basil, oregano, or other herbs

broccoli

Canadian bacon

chicken

green or black olives

green or sweet red peppers

mushrooms

onions

pepperoni

pineapple

roasted garlic

spinach

Biscuit Tortoni / *Tortoni*

¾ c. chilled whipping cream*

3 tbsp. sugar

½ c. almond macaroon cookie crumbs

1 tsp. almond extract

2 tbsp. chopped maraschino cherries

¼ c. chopped toasted almonds (optional)

1. Line 6 muffin or custard cups with paper cupcake liners.

2. Beat whipping cream and sugar in a chilled bowl until stiff.

3. Set aside 2 tbsp. macaroon crumbs. Fold rest of crumbs, almond extract, cherries, and almonds into whipped cream.

4. Spoon mixture into prepared cups and sprinkle with remaining crumbs. Cover with aluminum foil or plastic wrap and freeze until firm (about 4 hours).

Preparation time: 20 minutes
Chilling time: 4 hours
Serves 6

*For a lighter version of Biscuit Tortoni, substitute 2½ to 3 c. softened low-fat or nonfat frozen yogurt for the whipping cream and sugar. Skip step 2 and simply fold the macaroon mixture into the frozen yogurt. Good yogurt flavors to try are vanilla, chocolate, or coffee.

First created in southern Italy, tortoni is a tasty chilled dessert that is ideal for hot weather.

Holiday and Festival Food

A meal is always an important occasion in Italy, but holiday and festival meals are truly major events. Although in modern times extended family does not always live under one roof, as was common in the past, Italian families still try hard to be together for celebrations. Friends also visit each other during the holidays to share treats and good wishes. Since the company and the conversation are just as important as the food itself, these gatherings may easily last for hours.

The following recipes all have special connections to particular holidays or festivals, but many of them are also eaten year-round in Italy. Prepare these dishes for special occasions or when you're just feeling festive. And be sure to enjoy them the Italian way—take your time and don't rush!

Many small towns in Italy serve up bruschetta at olive festivals in late fall. What better way to celebrate? (Recipe on page 60.)

Bruschetta

Although basic bruschetta is a traditional treat at autumn olive festivals, it is easy to adapt this dish to any season. Tomatoes and basil make the following version summery, but try using hearty mushrooms in the fall, marinated black olives or artichoke hearts in the winter, or bright asparagus in the spring.

3 ripe red tomatoes

2 cloves garlic, finely chopped

⅓ c. chopped fresh basil

⅓ c. chopped fresh parsley

½ tsp. salt

½ tsp. pepper

⅓ c. olive oil

8 ½-inch-thick slices of
   crusty Italian or French bread

1. Preheat oven to 400°F.

2. Chop tomatoes and remove as many seeds as possible.

3. Combine all ingredients except bread with the tomatoes and set aside.

4. Place bread slices on a cookie sheet and toast in the oven for about 5 minutes. Turn slices over with a spatula and toast for another 5 minutes, or until golden brown. Remove from oven and place slices on a serving plate.

5. Spoon tomato mixture over toasted bread and serve immediately.

Preparation time: 10 minutes
Cooking time: 10 minutes
Serves 4

Linguine with Pesto/*Linguine al Pesto*

This simple but tasty dish is one you might find at Pontedassio's *Sagra del Basilico* (Basil Festival).

1 lb. linguine, uncooked

3 large garlic cloves

⅓ c. olive oil

1½ c. loosely packed fresh
    basil leaves (whole)

⅔ c. grated Parmesan cheese

½ tsp. salt

½ tsp. pepper

1. Cook linguine al dente, following directions on package. Before draining, carefully scoop out ⅓ c. of pasta cooking water with a measuring cup and set aside. Drain the pasta.

2. While pasta is cooking, coarsely chop the garlic. In a food processor or blender, combine olive oil, garlic, and basil. Process until you have a moist, well-mixed paste. Transfer paste to a small bowl and stir in Parmesan cheese, salt, pepper, and pasta cooking water. This is your pesto.*

3. In a large serving bowl, combine pesto and linguine, toss well, and serve.

Preparation time: 15 minutes
Cooking time: 15 to 20 minutes
Serves 4 to 6

*This is a basic pesto, but there are countless variations on the standard recipe. Add ¼ c. toasted pine nuts, ¼ c. lemon juice, or ⅔ c. fresh parsley when blending to change the flavor of your pesto.

Hot Cross Buns

Many Italians enjoy hot cross buns on Good Friday and over Easter weekend, but they make a good treat any time of the year.

Dough:

1 package refrigerated
    crescent rolls

⅓ c. raisins

¼ tsp. grated lemon peel
    or orange peel (optional)

Icing ingredients:

¼ c. powdered sugar

1½ tsp. milk

¼ tsp. vanilla extract

1. Preheat oven to 375°F.

2. Remove dough according to directions on package. Separate rolls into 8 triangles.

3. In a small bowl, combine raisins and lemon or orange peel. (If you are only using raisins, this step is not necessary.)

4. Place about 1 tsp. of raisin mixture in the center of each triangle. Roll up each triangle and pinch the edges to seal. Place rolls on an ungreased cookie sheet and bake 12 to 14 minutes or until golden brown.

5. Remove and place rolls on a cooling rack. In a small bowl, combine powdered sugar, milk, and vanilla extract. Stir until smooth, adding up to ½ tsp. more milk if necessary.

6. Drizzle icing in a cross shape on top of each bun and serve.

Preparation time: 20 to 25 minutes
Baking time: 10 to 15 minutes
Makes 8 buns

Rice and Pea Risotto/*Risi e Bisi*

6 tbsp. unsalted butter

¾ c. finely chopped onion

1½ c. rice, uncooked

4½ c. chicken broth, heated

2 c. fresh peas or 1 10-oz. package frozen peas, thawed

salt and pepper to taste

1 tbsp. finely chopped fresh parsley

½ c. grated Parmesan cheese

1. Heat 4 tbsp. of the butter in a large saucepan over medium heat. When it is sizzling, stir in onion, reduce heat to low, and cook, stirring constantly, for 5 minutes.

2. Add rice and cook, stirring occasionally, until the rice is no longer see-through.

3. Add ½ c. of the broth and cook, stirring, for about 2 minutes.

4. Add peas, 2 c. of broth, salt, and pepper. Cover, raise heat to high, and bring to a boil. Reduce heat to medium and cook, stirring occasionally with a fork, until all of the broth is absorbed.

5. Add 1 c. of broth. When this is absorbed, add the last of the broth and cook until the rice and peas are tender (probably about 15 to 20 minutes).

6. Add parsley, Parmesan cheese, and the remaining butter. Mix lightly and serve immediately in soup bowls.

Preparation time: 10 minutes
Cooking time: 1 hour
Serves 6

Risi e bisi *is a mouth-watering combination of creamy rice and bright spring peas.*

Stuffed Pasta in Broth / *Tortellini in Brodo*

Tortellini can be stuffed with meat, cheese, or even some types of vegetables such as spinach or mushrooms. Any kind of filling will work for this dish.

2 14½-oz. cans vegetable broth*

9 oz. fresh or frozen tortellini

¼ c. chopped fresh parsley

½ c. grated Parmesan cheese

pepper to taste

1. Bring the broth to a boil over high heat. Add the tortellini and lower heat to medium. Cook, stirring occasionally, for about 7 minutes, or until the tortellini are tender but still firm.

2. Divide the soup among 4 individual bowls. Sprinkle each serving with parsley, Parmesan cheese, and pepper. Serve hot.

Preparation time: 10 minutes
Cooking time: 7 to 10 minutes
Serves 4

*Some cooks like to liven up this simple soup by adding ingredients to the broth. Try adding a cup of frozen peas at the same time that you add the tortellini. Or, in the last two or three minutes of cooking, add one 14½-oz. can of stewed tomatoes or a thawed and drained package of frozen spinach. For a spicier dish, sauté a chopped medium onion or a minced clove of garlic and add it to the broth before boiling.

Dead Bone Cookies/*Ossi dei Morti*

These crunchy little cookies get their name from their resemblance to bones. On All Souls' Day, many Italian families bake them at home or buy them at shops and markets.

⅔ c. sugar

8 tbsp. unsalted butter

2 eggs

2 c. sifted all-purpose flour

1 tsp. vanilla extract

1 c. ground almonds or
   pistachios (optional)

1. Preheat oven to 400°F.

2. Lightly grease 2 cookie sheets.

3. Combine sugar, butter, and eggs in a medium-sized bowl. Add the flour gradually, beating until smooth. Add the vanilla and nuts and mix well.

4. Break off small pieces of dough (about 1 tbsp. each), and form them into skinny, bonelike shapes. Place them 1 inch apart on the cookie sheets.

5. Bake 10 minutes or until the cookies are lightly browned. Remove from cookie sheets with a spatula and cool on a wire rack.

Preparation time: 20 to 25 minutes
Baking time: 10 to 15 minutes
Makes about 2 dozen cookies

Ossi dei morti *are simple to make and fun to eat! Try serving them with hot chocolate or coffee for a sweet snack.*

Index

About the Author

Alphonse "Babe" Bisignano was born in Des Moines, Iowa, to an Italian family who originally came from the region of Calabria in southern Italy. Bisignano became a boxer at the age of 16, and at 18 he won the Iowa light-heavyweight championship. He then went to New York and became a professional wrestler.

Bisignano returned to Iowa in 1939 and opened Babe's Restaurant in downtown Des Moines. The restaurant, which featured Italian and American food, was a popular Des Moines eating establishment for over fifty years. Bisignano is retired and lives in Des Moines.

Photo Acknowledgments
The photographs in this book are reproduced courtesy of: © Chuck Place, pp. 2–3; © Robert L. & Diane Wolfe, pp. 4 (both), 6, 18, 34, 38, 57; © Walter, Louiseann Pietrowicz/September 8th Stock, pp. 5 (both), 30, 41, 42, 45, 46, 48, 51, 58, 62, 65, 66, 69; © 2000 Elizabeth Buie. All Rights Reserved, pp. 10, 16; © AFP/CORBIS, p. 13; © Robert Fried/Robert Fried Photography, p. 26.

Cover photos: © Chuck Place, front top; © Walter, Louiseann Pietrowicz/September 8th Stock, front bottom, spine; © Robert L. & Diane Wolfe, back.

The illustrations on pp. 7, 19, 27, 29, 31, 33, 35, 40, 43, 47, 49, 50, 53, 54, 56, 59, 61, and 67 and the map on p. 8 are by Tim Seeley.